Why should I recycle rubbish?

one small step

M J Knight

PLÁSTICO

LATA

VIDRO

W
FRANKLIN WATTS
LONDON•SYDNEY

An Appleseed Editions book

First published in 2008 by Franklin Watts
338 Euston Road, London NW1 3BH

Franklin Watts Australia
Hachette Children's Books
Level 17/207 Kent St, Sydney, NSW 2000

© 2008 Appleseed Editions

Created by Appleseed Editions Ltd,
Well House, Friars Hill, Guestling,
East Sussex TN35 4ET

Designed by Guy Callaby
Edited by Jinny Johnson
Illustrations by Hel James
Picture research by Su Alexander

ISBN 978 07496 8048 0

Dewey Classification: 363.72' 82.

A CIP catalogue for this book is available from the British Library.

Picture acknowledgements
Title Page Paulo Fridman/Corbis; 4 Stuart McCall/Getty Images;
6 Anne Domdey/Corbis; 7 Michael S. Lewis/Corbis; 9 Gary Bell/
Zefa/Corbis; 10 Louise Murray/Getty Images; 12 Roger Wood/
Corbis; 14 Paulo Fridman/Corbis; 16 Nick Vedros & Assoc./Getty
Images; 19 Lester Lefkowitz/Corbis; 21 Allan H. Shoemake/Getty
Images; 22 James L. Amos/Corbis; 24 Randy Faris/Corbis;
26 Gari Wyn Williams/Alamy; 28 Don Smith/Alamy.
Front cover: Gary Buss/Getty Images

Printed in China

Franklin Watts is a division of Hachette Children's Books

Contents

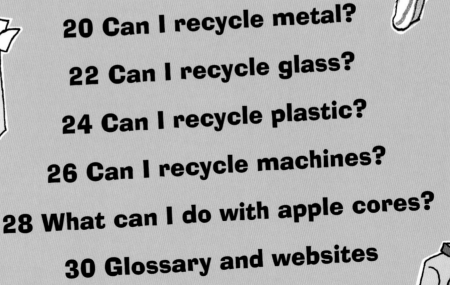

A mountain of rubbish

Every year we throw away more rubbish than we did the year before. Even just in the UK people chuck away more than 100 million tonnes of rubbish every year.

If we keep on throwing away this much rubbish we are going to run out of places to put it. So everyone needs to stop and think about how to make less rubbish.

There are twice as many people in the world now as 100 years ago, and we all throw away lots of rubbish.

What is recycling?

One way to make less rubbish is to use things again instead of throwing them away. This is called recycling. Plastic bags are easy to recycle. You can use them again for your shopping or put them in a special recycling bin to be made into new ones. Making plastic bags from recycled plastic uses much less energy than making them from scratch.

A step in the right direction

You might think that what you do doesn't matter, but it does. It matters very much. Every time you recycle a glass jar or use a plastic bag again instead of taking a new one you take a step in the right direction. You can make a difference – everyone can. If lots of people take a step in the right direction, even a small one, these small steps will add up to one big step.

That's rubbish!

What do you do when you don't want something any more? You throw it away – it's rubbish. Rubbish can be anything from a sweet wrapper to a broken toy.

At home we throw away leftover food, packaging, paper, cans and bottles. This is called household waste. The rubbish that shops, offices, factories and schools throw away is called industrial and commercial waste.

About one-fifth of the rubbish in our dustbins is food we have thrown away.

Cleaning up Everest

You would think that Mount Everest, the world's highest mountain, would be a very clean place, with no rubbish. But climbers have left lots of junk such as cans, old tents, food and medicine behind them over the years. A Japanese climber called Ken Noguchi has been cleaning up Mount Everest. He has made five trips to the peak with some other climbers. They have collected a total of 9,000 kilos of rubbish!

Rubbish can be dangerous

Some rubbish can harm people, animals and the world around us. Harmful rubbish includes things such as batteries, paint and electrical equipment. We all need to be very careful about where and how we throw these things away.

Too much rubbish

Households throw away 31 million tonnes of rubbish every year – half a tonne for every person! That much rubbish weighs the same as three and a half million double-decker buses, which would stretch round the world two and half times.

Lots of things we throw away could be useful to someone else – from furniture to toys.

One small fact

The rubbish every household throws away each year weighs as much as a teenage elephant!

I can make a difference

Check out your family's rubbish. How many bags of rubbish did your household throw out this week?

Count how many plastic or glass bottles and cans your family recycle and check how much paper or card you recycle.

Is there anything else in the rubbish that you could reuse or recycle?

A load of rubbish

The biggest waste dump in the world is floating on the Pacific Ocean. The Great Pacific Garbage Patch is nearly four times the size of Great Britain. Almost all the rubbish in the patch is floating plastic.

What happens to our rubbish?

Most of the rubbish we put out every week is picked up by dustbin trucks. They take the rubbish to tips, where it is buried in the ground.

Tips are also called landfill sites. About three-quarters of rubbish goes into tips. The UK buries more waste than any other country in Europe, except for Greece, which buries about 90 per cent of its rubbish. In the UK a small amount of rubbish is burned at very high temperatures in a furnace. Denmark and Sweden burn more than half of their rubbish.

A tipper truck empties out a load of rubbish in a landfill site near London.

One small fact

Everyone throws away their own weight in rubbish every seven weeks.

Think about the different kinds of rubbish in your bin. Some, such as paper, food leftovers and grass cuttings, rot away after a while. This kind of rubbish is called biodegradable. Other kinds never rot, however long you leave them for. This type of rubbish includes bottles and cans.

Biodegradable

Non-biodegradable

A step in the right direction

One way to make less rubbish is to buy fewer things, or buy things with less packaging. When you help with the shopping, try to find food that does not have lots of wrapping. Look for fruit and vegetables that are sold loose instead of in plastic trays.

Market stalls are great places to buy food which doesn't have a lot of packaging. This stall in a market in Pakistan sells fresh fruits and nuts.

I can make a difference

Do you bring a packed lunch to school? Is the food wrapped in packaging that you throw away? Cut down on the rubbish from your packed lunch by bringing it in a plastic box that you can use every day. Ask your mum and dad to buy a reusable bottle for drinks so you don't have drink cartons, cans or bottles to throw away.

Reuse carrier bags

Remind everyone to take cloth bags or strong carrier bags when you go shopping. You can use these over and over again, so you won't need lots of other plastic bags for shopping.

Help your mum and dad by looking out for items such as toilet rolls and kitchen rolls made from recycled paper. Buying these means that you are using less of the things that are needed to make them.

One small fact

Twenty years ago every home threw away about 397 kilos of rubbish every year. Only three kilos of this were recycled. Two years ago every home threw 517 kilos of rubbish every year, but 113 kilos of this were recycled.

What can I recycle?

Think before you throw anything in the bin. Lots of things can be recycled, such as paper, plastic and glass bottles, cans, grass cuttings and much more. It helps you remember to recycle if you keep a special bin or box next to the dustbin.

It's easy to recycle when recycling bins are different coloured and clearly labelled like this row of bins in Brazil.

Can I use these again?

Look at the pictures and write down on a piece of scrap paper the ones you can think can be recycled. Answers on page 32.

Find out the best way to recycle. In some areas you can put rubbish for recycling into special boxes or bags, which the bin men bring. These are collected at a different time from the rest of the rubbish. Or you can take things for recycling to a centre where there are big bins for glass, cans, paper and other things.

See if you can find any clothes and toys you don't want any more. Take them to a charity shop so other people can use them. If you have a garden, you can put your garden waste in a special bin. It rots down into a kind of earth called compost and can be put on the soil to help the plants grow.

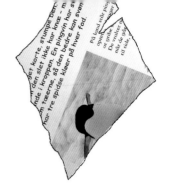

Piles and piles of paper

Most of us have so much paper, but there is no need to throw away newspapers, magazines, junk mail, cardboard or even your old homework! It is easy to recycle most of the paper we use.

Find out if your school has a paper recycling scheme. If it does, get together with friends and see if you can find out how often the paper is collected and where it goes. If your school doesn't recycle paper yet, ask if you can start.

One small fact

Every tonne of paper recycled saves 17 trees

I can make a difference

Keep a box at home for recycled paper. It could be a cardboard box or a special box or bag from the local council. Every time you finish with a comic or a magazine, put it in the box. If you have been using paper for a project, put all the leftover pieces in the box. When the box is full, help your mum and dad take it to a paper recycling bin. Or put it out to be collected on the day your local recycling team comes round.

Every person uses more than 200 kilos of paper every year. More than half of this is recycled.

How is paper recycled?

The paper we put into recycling bins is sorted and then taken to a place called a paper mill. It is made into pulp and washed. Any staples and glue are taken out. Then the pulp is put into a tank like a giant washing machine where soap removes the ink from the paper.

1. Waste paper is sorted

2. Sorted paper is pulped

5. Clean pulp is dried and rolled into sheets

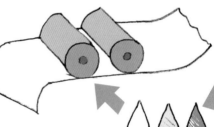

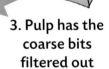

4. Pulp is washed, and ink is removed

3. Pulp has the coarse bits filtered out

I can make a difference

Think about cutting down the amount of paper you use and throw away. Always use both sides of a piece of paper.

Keep a box of paper pieces to use for scribbling notes.

Unwrap presents carefully so that you can use the wrapping paper again. Cut pictures out of cards you are sent or use colourful paper to make your own greetings cards.

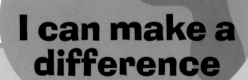

The washed paper goes into an enormous machine. The machine squeezes the water out between two wire meshes and winds the dry paper on to enormous reels. The reels are sent to printers to be turned into new newspapers and magazines.

Each of these huge reels of paper weighs several tonnes.

New paper from old

● A fifth of everything we put out for recycling is paper and card.

● A paper recycling machine makes two kilometres of paper a minute.

● Old newspapers and magazines can be recycled into new ones in only seven days.

Can I recycle metal?

Yes. Recycled metal is every bit as good as new metal, so it can be used over and over again. Recycling uses just a tiny bit of the energy needed to make new metal so it saves lots of energy.

Cans are made from steel or aluminium. Both types are made from strips of metal formed into can shapes. They are coated with lacquer to stop them going rusty. Recycling aluminium costs less than recycling almost any other material.

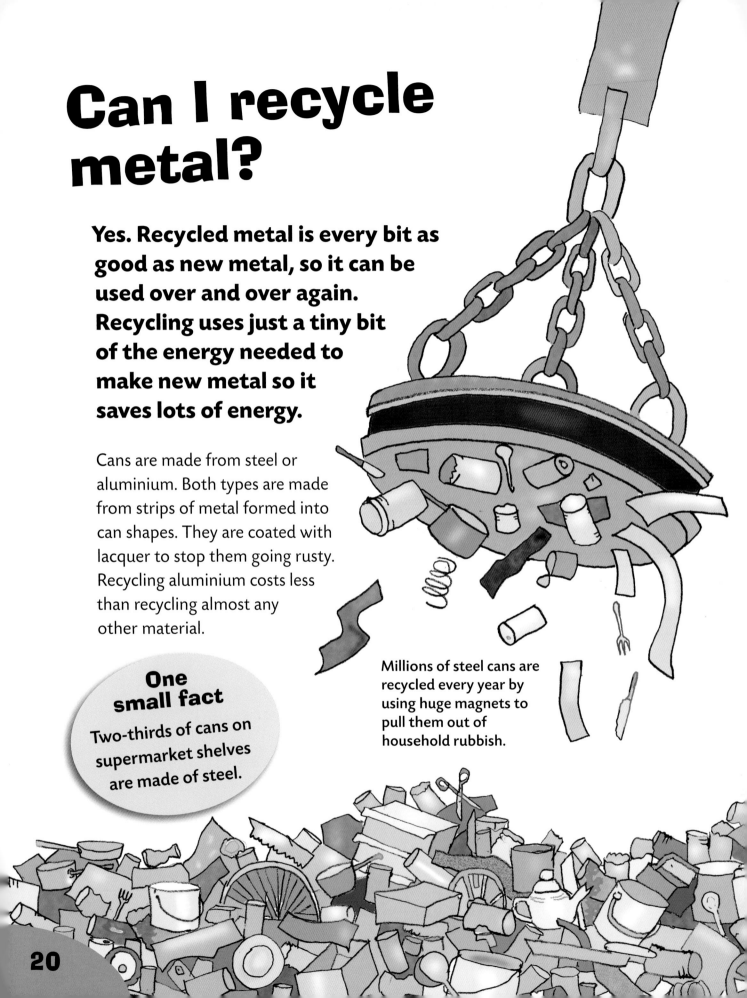

One small fact

Two-thirds of cans on supermarket shelves are made of steel.

Millions of steel cans are recycled every year by using huge magnets to pull them out of household rubbish.

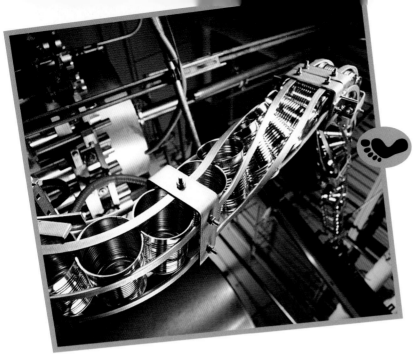

Recycling a steel can uses just a quarter of the energy needed to make a completely new one. Every household uses 600 steel cans a year but only half of them are recycled.

● Recycling one aluminium can saves enough energy to run a TV for three hours.

● Recycling one steel can saves enough energy to power a 60-watt light bulb for nearly four hours.

I can make a difference

Not enough people recycle their cans. Can you think of ways to change this?

Does your school have a bin for recycled cans? If not you could write to your local council to ask for one.

Why not have a collect-a-can week with a prize for the team that brings in the most cans to recycle.

You could also collect washed, used foil for recycling.

You can too!

American president George Bush gave one Californian school a special award for recycling. Every Friday children took in cans from home to recycle. The children asked their neighbours and local companies to help recycle too. They collected thousands of aluminium drink cans, soup cans and plastic bottles and raised money for new playground equipment by selling them.

Can I recycle glass?

Glass can be recycled again and again. It is impossible to tell whether a glass bottle is newly made or recycled.

Empty glass jars and bottles are called cullet. They are sorted by colour, such as green, brown and clear. The glass is then crushed, mixed with raw materials and melted at a high heat in a furnace. The melted glass is used to make new bottles or jars.

A tractor moves huge piles of crushed green glass at a glass recycling plant in West Virginia in the USA.

One small fact

A bottle bank can hold up to 3000 bottles before it needs to be emptied.

In the UK we recycle about half the glass bottles and jars we use. This is double the amount we recycled five years ago. Some countries such as Switzerland and Finland recycle more than 90 per cent of the glass they use.

Saving energy?

Making glass bottles and jars from recycled ones saves loads of energy. Just recycling one glass bottle saves enough energy to run a computer for 20 minutes.

Recycled glass can be used for lots of things – even resurfacing roads. About 14 million glass bottles were crushed and used to resurface a motorway in Britain.

Can I recycle plastic?

Millions of plastic bottles are recycled every year. Most plastic is made from oil, and there are about 50 types of plastic.

Before they can be recycled plastic bottles have to be sorted into the different types. Then the bottles are washed and broken into tiny flakes. When these have dried, they can be used to make new things.

One small fact

Every household uses 373 plastic bottles every year, but recycles only 29.

24

I can make a difference

If everyone in the country stopped taking plastic bags in shops there would be 7.8 billion fewer plastic bags thrown away every year. So why don't you make a start? Maybe your family and friends will copy you.

What can be made?

Lots of different things can be made out of plastic bottles and other items.

● Fizzy drink and cooking oil bottles can be made into sleeping bags and anoraks, new packaging, wall and floor coverings and fleecy clothing. It takes about 25 two-litre bottles to make one fleece jacket.

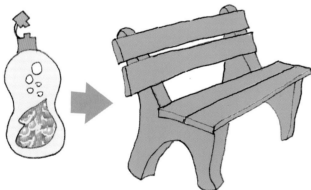

● Containers for fruit juice, washing-up liquid and fabric conditioner can be made into fences, park benches and signposts. These bottles can also be refilled and used again and again.

● Mineral water, squash and shampoo bottles, as well as plastic food trays and cling film, can be made into drainage pipes, electrical fittings and clothing.

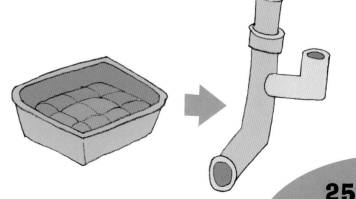

Can I recycle machines?

Lots of machines can be recycled or passed on to someone else when we have finished with them.

A mobile phone should work for five years. But lots of people get a new one every year because they want the latest kind. Mobile phones contain a chemical called cadmium. Each one contains enough cadmium to pollute, or spoil, 600,000 litres of water when it is thrown away. You can take old mobile phones to charities, which can update and reuse them.

People in Europe throw away nearly 100 million mobile phones every year. Most could be recycled or reused.

One small fact

We throw away more than six million electrical items every year.

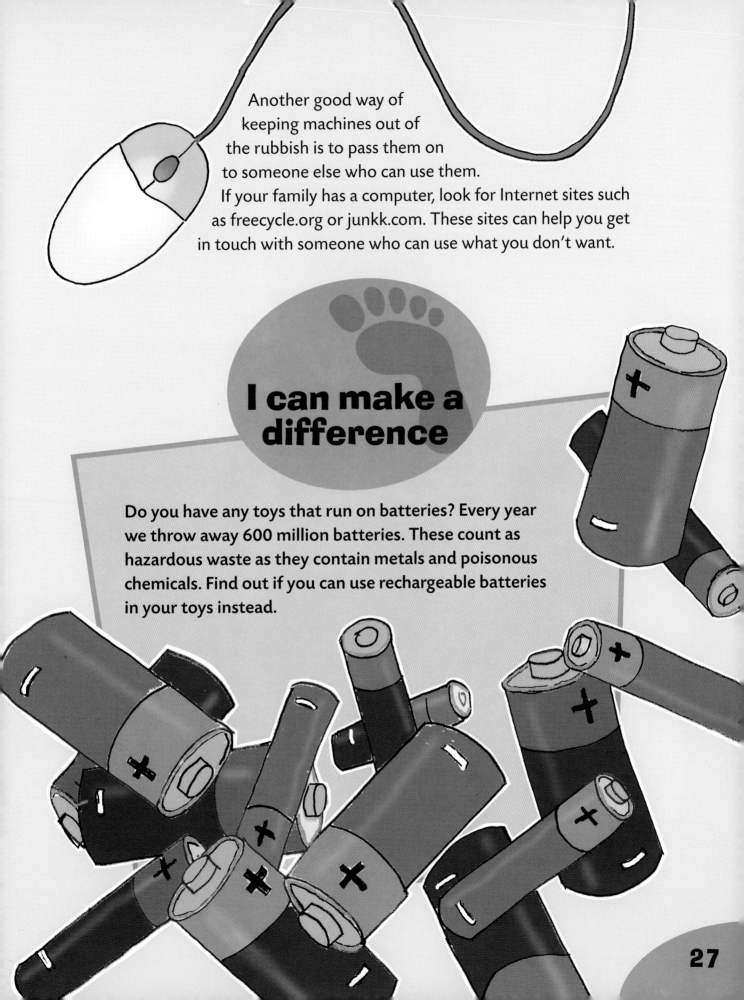

Another good way of keeping machines out of the rubbish is to pass them on to someone else who can use them. If your family has a computer, look for Internet sites such as freecycle.org or junkk.com. These sites can help you get in touch with someone who can use what you don't want.

I can make a difference

Do you have any toys that run on batteries? Every year we throw away 600 million batteries. These count as hazardous waste as they contain metals and poisonous chemicals. Find out if you can use rechargeable batteries in your toys instead.

What can I do with apple cores?

Almost a quarter of the rubbish we put in our bins is plant waste, such as vegetable and fruit peelings, grass cuttings and weeds.

When plant material is thrown away in a landfill site, it makes a harmful liquid called leachate. This is bad for water and soil. The best thing to do with plant waste is to put it all in a compost bin. It slowly rots down and can then be put on the garden to help plants grow. Always wash your hands after using the compost bin.

One small fact

It takes nine months to a year for your plant waste to turn into moist brown compost that can be put on the garden.

 Leftover fresh fruit and vegetables are perfect for making compost.

✔ Put these in your compost heap ✔

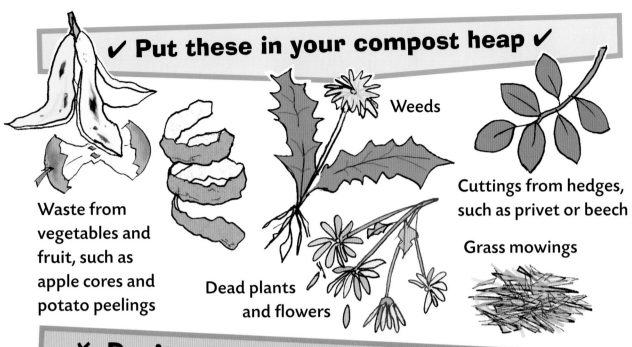

Weeds

Cuttings from hedges, such as privet or beech

Grass mowings

Waste from vegetables and fruit, such as apple cores and potato peelings

Dead plants and flowers

✗ Don't put these in your compost heap ✗

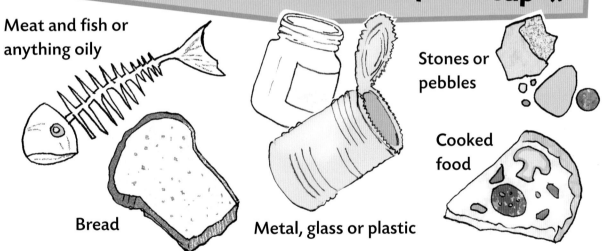

Meat and fish or anything oily

Stones or pebbles

Cooked food

Bread

Metal, glass or plastic

Help your family or school to start composting. You will need a compost bin with a lid, and plastic buckets to collect the compost. Find an out-of-the-way corner and put your compost bin on grass or bare soil, not on concrete or tarmac.

I can make a difference

Glossary

aluminium
A very light, silvery-grey metal. Most drinks cans are made from aluminium.

biodegradable
Biodegradable rubbish will rot away after a while if it is thrown away. Fruit and grass cuttings are biodegradable. Non-biodegradable rubbish, such as cans and plastic, will never rot.

bottle bank
A place where you can take empty glass bottles and jars to recycle them.

compost
Rotted down plant and food waste which can be turned into plant food in a compost heap.

hazardous waste
Things people have thrown away which may contain dangerous chemicals, such as batteries or paint.

lacquer
A liquid that dries to make a smooth shiny coating and stops metal cans from going rusty.

landfill site
A place where rubbish is dumped and usually buried.

pulp
A soft, shapeless, wet pile of material. Paper is made from a pulp of fibres.

rechargeable battery
A rechargeable battery can be used again and again. When the battery runs out of energy it can be plugged into a socket and refilled with energy.

recycling
Recycling is using things again. Many things and materials can be used and then reused, from scraps of paper to mobile phones.

Websites

http://www.recyclenow.com
Useful information on how things are made and how you can recycle just about anything.

http://www.eco-schools.org/
Eco-Schools programme, which schools can join if they want to help look after the environment.

http://www.recycle-more.co.uk/
Ideas and information about recycling.

http://www.gardenorganic.org.uk/schools_organic_network/index.php
Advice on starting a school garden and compost heap.

http://www.yellow-woods.co.uk/pages/kidskabin
A website for children with quizzes and activities related to recycling and the environment.

http://www.fones4schools.co.uk/default.aspx
This website tells children and teachers how to collect and recycle old mobile phones, and raise money for the school at the same time.

Index

Can I use these again? (see page 15)

Can be recycled at most recycling centres

newspapers   cereal boxes
glass bottles   plastic milk bottles
comics   apple cores
egg boxes   cans

Can be recycled, but not everywhere

orange-juice cartons   yoghurt pots

Can be recycled through charity shops or websites

televisions   toy cars   dolls

Can't be recycled

crisp packets
empty felt-tipped pens
batteries (unless rechargeable)

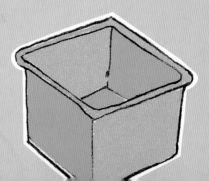